dabblelab

SOCK PUPPET THEATER PRESENTS

Goldilocks
and the
Three
Bears

A Make and Play Production

by Christopher L. Harbo

CAPSTONE PRESS
a capstone imprint

Dabble Lab Books are published by Capstone Press,
1710 Roe Crest Drive, North Mankato, Minnesota 56003
www.mycapstone.com

Cataloging-in-Publication Data is available at the Library of Congress website.
ISBN: 978-1-5157-6681-0 (library binding)
ISBN: 978-1-5157-6685-8 (eBook PDF)

Editorial Credits
Juliette Peters, designer; Marcy Morin, puppet and prop creator;
Sarah Schuette, photo stylist; Morgan Walters, media researcher;
Tori Abraham, production specialist

Photo Credits
All photos by Capstone studio, Karon Dubke with the exception of: Shutterstock: Eric Isselee, 4, Mammut Vision, design element throughout, Matt Gibson, 5, Ondrej83, 19, Pattern image, design element throughout, photocell, design element throughout, Reshavskyi, design element throughout, Yomka, design element throughout

Printed in Canada.
010395F17

About the Author

Christopher L. Harbo grew up watching *Sesame Street*, *Mister Rogers' Neighborhood*, and *The Muppet Show*. Ever since then, he's wanted to be a puppeteer — and now his dream has finally come true! In addition to puppetry, Christopher enjoys folding origami, reading comic books, and watching superhero movies.

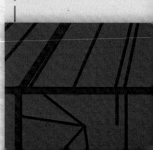

Table of Contents

Goldilocks and the Three Bears

The story of Goldilocks dates back to Robert Southey's 1837 tale *The Story of the Three Bears.* In that version, an old woman invades the three bears' home. After many retellings, the tale changed. By 1904 the little girl we know as Goldilocks became its star for good.

Now you can tell your own version of *Goldilocks and the Three Bears* with puppets. The pages to come present dozens of ideas for creating and performing a complete sock puppet production. You'll find simple instructions for making the puppets, stage, and props. You'll also discover a full play script and helpful performance tips. So don't wait another second. Flex your fingers. It's time to bring your sock puppets to life!

The Plot

The story begins with a baby bear, a mama bear, and a papa bear who live in a house in the woods. One morning, the bears make porridge and go for a walk to give the food time to cool.

Soon a golden-haired child named Goldilocks comes to the house. She walks right in and sees the porridge on the table. Goldilocks tries the porridge from the big bowl — it's too hot. Next she tastes the medium bowl — it's too cold. Finally she tries the little bowl. It's just right, so she gobbles it up!

Next Goldilocks tries out the bears' chairs. Only Baby Bear's chair feels just right, and she sits in it until it breaks. Then Goldilocks lies in the bears' beds. Once again, only Baby Bear's bed feels just right. The child falls fast asleep.

When the bears return, they discover someone's been eating their porridge, sitting in their chairs, and sleeping in their beds. Then Baby Bear exclaims, "Someone's been sleeping in my bed — and here she is!"

Goldilocks awakes with a start. She hops out of bed, jumps out a window, and is never seen again.

The Cast

Goldilocks

Goldilocks is a bit of a troublemaker. She has no problem, whatsoever, waltzing right into the three bears' house uninvited. She also doesn't think twice about using, and abusing, their things.

Baby Bear

Baby Bear is a kind-hearted, gentle creature. He can't understand why anyone would want to steal his breakfast or break his chair. Pulling a stunt like Goldilocks does is beyond his wildest imagination.

Mama Bear

Mama Bear is a loving mother who knows how to solve problems when they arise. She is sensible and practical but also stern when she needs to be. As Goldilocks discovers in the end, you don't mess with Mama!

Papa Bear

Papa Bear is the cook of the family. Nothing makes him happier than fixing a big batch of his famous porridge. If Papa has one flaw, it's that he's a wee-bit careless. He often forgets to lock the front door when the family goes for walks.

Yoo-hoo! Is anyone home?

Supplies to Create
Goldilocks

- large tan sock
- 3.25-inch (8.3-cm) foam half ball
- cardboard
- pencil
- scissors
- craft glue
- ruler
- yellow yarn
- 2 bows
- googly eyes
- pink bead
- pink felt
- large pink sock

1. Turn the tan sock inside out.

2. Place the flat side of the foam half ball on the cardboard. Trace around the base of the ball with a pencil.

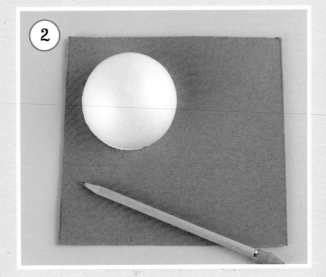

3. Cut out the circle traced on the cardboard.

4. Fold the cardboard circle in half.

5. Glue one side of the folded cardboard to the base of the foam half ball. Line up the curve of the cardboard with the curved edge of the ball. The loose flap of cardboard will form the mouth of the puppet.

6. Apply glue inside the top and bottom of the mouth. Tuck the toe of the sock into the mouth and allow the glue to dry.

7. Turn the sock right side out, pulling it over the foam half ball.

8. Cut 20 18-inch- (46-centimeter-) long pieces of yarn. Group them lengthwise on the table.

9. Cut one 6-inch- (15-cm-) long piece of yarn. Tie it around the center of the long group of yarn to form hair. Trim off any excess yarn after the knot.

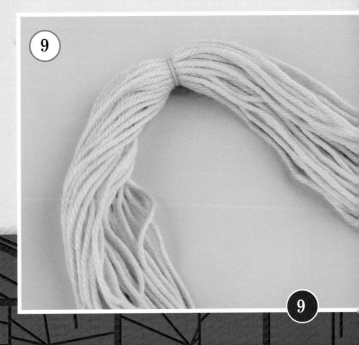

10. Glue the hair to the top of the puppet's head. Center the hair on the knot made in step 9.

11. Cut five 3-inch- (8-cm-) long pieces of yarn. Lay them side-by-side on the table.

12. Cut one 3-inch- (8-cm-) long piece of yarn. Lay it across the center of the five pieces of yarn.

13. Fold the five pieces of yarn in half over the single piece of yarn. Then tie the single piece of yarn to the hair on top of the puppet to make bangs. Trim off any excess string after the knot.

14. Cut two 3-inch- (8-cm-) long pieces of yarn. Tie one on each side of the puppet's hair to form pigtails. Trim off any excess yarn after the knots.

15. Glue bows on top of the pigtail ties to hide them.

16. Glue googly eyes to the puppet's head.

17. Glue the bead below the eyes to make a nose.

18. Cut a small half-moon shape out of pink felt. Glue it inside the mouth to form a tongue.

19. Cut the toe off the pink sock. Slide the sock onto Goldilocks' body to serve as a dress.

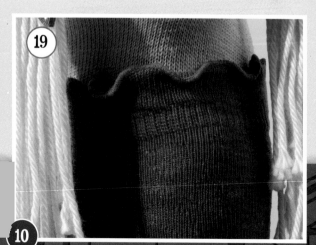

Supplies to Create

The Three Bears

- 3 large brown socks
- 3 3.25-inch (8.3-cm) foam half balls
- cardboard
- pencil
- scissors
- craft glue
- dark brown felt
- light brown felt
- 6 googly eyes
- pink felt
- 3 brown pom-poms
- bow
- toy pearl necklace
- green felt

I'm just a wee baby bear, yes-sir-ee.

Baby Bear

1. Turn the sock inside out.

2. Place the flat side of the foam half ball on the cardboard. Trace around the base of the ball with a pencil.

3. Cut out the circle traced on the cardboard.

4. Fold the cardboard circle in half.

5. Glue one side of the folded cardboard to the base of the foam half ball. Line up the curve of the cardboard with the curved edge of the ball. The loose flap of cardboard will form the mouth of the puppet.

6. Apply glue inside the top and bottom of the mouth. Tuck the toe of the sock into the mouth and allow the glue to dry.

7. Turn the sock right side out, pulling it over the foam half ball.

8. Cut two ear shapes out of the dark brown felt. Set aside.

9. Cut two smaller ear shapes out of the light brown felt. Glue the light brown inner ears to the dark brown outer ears.

10. Glue the completed ears to the puppet's head.

11. Glue googly eyes to the puppet's head.

12. Cut a small half-moon shape out of pink felt. Glue it inside the mouth to form a tongue.

13. Glue a pom-pom nose below the eyes to finish Baby Bear.

Papa Bear

1. Repeat steps 1 to 13 from Baby Bear.

2. Cut a necktie shape out of the green felt.

3. Glue the necktie to the front of the puppet to complete Papa Bear.

We have an intruder!

Mama Bear

1. Repeat steps 1 to 13 from Baby Bear.

2. Glue a bow to the top of the puppet's head.

3. Fasten the toy pearl necklace around the puppet's neck to complete Mama Bear.

Search the whole house!

Stage and Prop Creation

Suggested Supplies:

- 4 long window curtains
- 3 tension rods
- doorway
- 2 ribbons
- scissors
- craft foam
- utility knife
- black marker
- felt
- craft glue
- craft sticks
- cardboard
- fabric

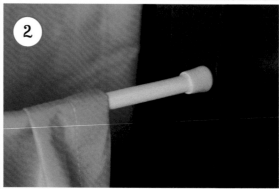

2

14

Stage:

1. Slide one curtain on a tension rod. Adjust the tension rod to fit a doorway. With an adult's help, hang the curtain from the top of the doorframe to create the back of the stage.

2. Adjust a second tension rod to fit the doorway and hang it about halfway up the frame. Drape a curtain over the tension rod to create the main stage.

3. Slide two curtains on the last tension rod. Adjust the rod and hang it in front of the curtain hung in step 1. Tie the curtains off to the sides with ribbon to frame the completed stage.

Porridge:

1. Use a scissors to cut three small eye shapes out of craft foam. Use different colors and make them slightly different sizes.

2. With an adult's help, use a utility knife to cut a slit across the top of each foam shape. Then use a black marker to outline the edges and slit to make the foam shapes look like bowls.

3. Cut three small circles out of felt. Slide the felt circles into the slits in the bowls to make porridge.

4. Glue craft sticks together into a three-pronged fork. Once dry, glue each bowl of porridge to a tine on the fork to complete the porridge prop.

15

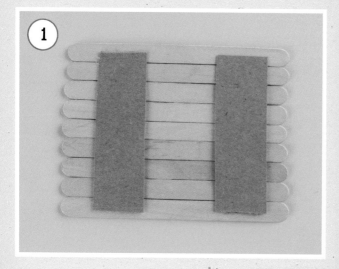

1

Chair:

1. Lay nine craft sticks side-by-side. Cut two strips of cardboard and glue them across the sticks to create a chair seat.

2. Glue craft sticks together to create the back and base of the chair. Use photo #2 as a guide.

3. Glue the chair seat from step 1 to the chair's base. Then glue four craft sticks to the base to create legs to complete the chair prop.

Broken Chair:

1. Glue 10 or so craft sticks together in a random pile.

2. Glue the pile of sticks to the end of a craft stick to complete the broken chair prop.

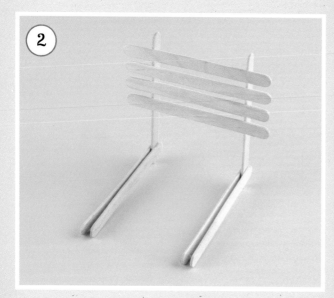

3

Bed:

1. Use a scissors to cut two long strips of cardboard. These will be the sideboards of the bed.

2. Cut a large headboard shape out of cardboard. Then cut a smaller footboard shape out of cardboard.

3. Glue the sideboards to the headboard and footboard to create a simple bed shape. The middle of the bed will be open to allow Goldilocks to slide in and out.

4. Use pieces of fabric to make blankets and even a pillow to complete the bed prop.

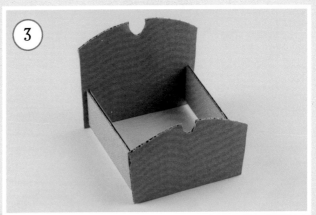

Now all I have is a pile of sticks!

Now that the stage is set, turn the page to read the script!

The Script

Narrator: Once upon a time, three kind and peaceful bears lived in a little house in the forest. There was a mama bear . . . *(Mama pops up)*

Mama: How do you do?

Narrator: . . . a papa bear . . . *(Papa pops up)*

Papa: Top of the morning to you!

Narrator: . . . and a baby bear *(Baby pops up)*

Baby: I'm just a wee baby bear, yes-sir-ee.

Narrator: Now on this day, Papa Bear had made a big pot of his famous porridge and served it up for his hungry family. *(three bowls pop up on stage)*

Papa: Breakfast is served! *(leans over his bowl)* Dig in.

Mama: Mmm . . . this looks so good, Papa.

Baby: Through my teeth and past my tongue, look out tummy here it comes!

(all three bears put their noses in the bowls)

Papa: Yowza! That's hot!

Mama: Yikes! It burns! It burns!

Baby: Whaaa! I can't feel my wee baby nose!

Papa: Ah, shucks. It looks like our porridge is much too hot to eat.

Baby: What are we going to do?

Mama: I know. It's such a fine day outside that we should go for a walk in the forest. By the time we return, our porridge will be cool enough to eat.

Papa: That's a great idea! Come on family, the great outdoors is calling!

(all three walk offstage, bowls leave stage)

Narrator: Not long after the three bears left the house, a little girl named Goldilocks came sulking through the forest. *(Goldilocks walks on stage)*

Goldilocks: Ugh! I'm so bored! There's nothing to do!

Narrator: Truth be told, Goldilocks was a rather naughty child. She had been so sassy to her mother that morning that she'd been sent outside to play — without her video games or cell phone — for the whole day.

Goldilocks: *(to audience)* Who are you calling sassy?! I don't have to put up with this! I'm out of here! *(walks offstage)*

Narrator: Yes . . . well . . . before long, the sass — I mean *spirited* — young lady came across the home of the three bears. Rather than knock, she barged right in to check out the place.

Goldilocks: *(peeking in from side of stage)* Yoo-hoo! Is anyone home?

Goldilocks: *(walking across stage)* Hmm . . . no answer. I guess I've got the place all to myself. He he he. Let's see if this house has Wi-Fi or something I can play with. *(bowls pop up on stage)*

Goldilocks: What's this! *(sniffs bowls)* Ugh! I hate porridge.

Goldilocks: But then again, I got sent outside without any breakfast — and I am kind of hungry. Perhaps I'll just taste it.

Goldilocks: *(dips her nose in big bowl)* Youch! This one's much too hot!

Goldilocks: *(dips her nose in medium bowl)* Eww! This one's much too cold!

Goldilocks: *(dips nose in small bowl, then gobbles hungrily)* Glug, glug, glug, glug.

Goldilocks: BUUURRPP! That one was just right! *(bowls duck down and small bowl's porridge is removed)*

Goldilocks: Oh, my! After such a heavy breakfast, I need to sit down. Let's see if this house has any comfy chairs. *(chair pops up)*

Goldilocks: Here's one! *(sits in chair)* Ugh! This chair is just way too big. *(hops off)*

(chair ducks down and pops up on the other side of Goldilocks)

Goldilocks: Maybe this one will be better. *(sits in chair)* Nope! This one is too lumpy! *(hops off)*

(chair ducks down and pops up on the other side of Goldilocks)

Goldilocks: Third time's a charm. *(sits in chair)* Ah! This one feels just right. Now I can kick back and relax. *(leans back in chair and falls backward and below stage)*

Sound Effect: CRASH!

Goldilocks: *(pops up)* Oh, dear. I think I broke it! No matter. Not my chair — not my problem.

Goldilocks: YAWN. All of this activity is making me tired. I bet the bedroom is upstairs. *(walks offstage)*

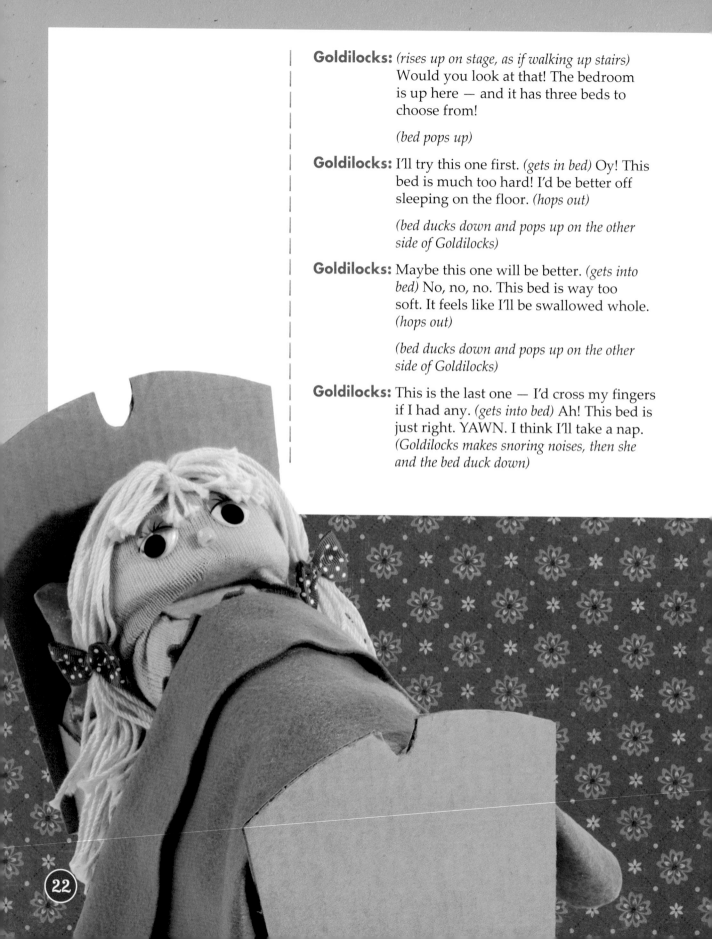

Goldilocks: *(rises up on stage, as if walking up stairs)* Would you look at that! The bedroom is up here — and it has three beds to choose from!

(bed pops up)

Goldilocks: I'll try this one first. *(gets in bed)* Oy! This bed is much too hard! I'd be better off sleeping on the floor. *(hops out)*

(bed ducks down and pops up on the other side of Goldilocks)

Goldilocks: Maybe this one will be better. *(gets into bed)* No, no, no. This bed is way too soft. It feels like I'll be swallowed whole. *(hops out)*

(bed ducks down and pops up on the other side of Goldilocks)

Goldilocks: This is the last one — I'd cross my fingers if I had any. *(gets into bed)* Ah! This bed is just right. YAWN. I think I'll take a nap. *(Goldilocks makes snoring noises, then she and the bed duck down)*

Narrator: Just as Goldilocks fell asleep, the three bears returned from their walk. *(three bears appear on stage)*

Mama: Home again, home again!

Papa: Yes, and by now our porridge should be just the right temperature to eat.

Baby: Yay! Let's dig in.

(three bowls pop up in front of bears)

Papa: *(looking down at his bowl)* What's this? Some of my porridge is missing. If I didn't know better, I'd say someone has been eating it!

Mama: *(looking down at her bowl)* You're not the only one. My bowl is half empty! I think someone's been eating my porridge as well!

Baby: *(looking down at his empty bowl)* Well at least you still have some. I know someone's been eating my porridge because it's all gone! WAAAAA!

Mama: This is terrible! Someone must have broken in while we were away! I wonder if anything else is amiss.

(chair pops up next to Papa)

Papa: *(sniffs chair)* Hmm . . . my chair smells funny. Like . . . like a human sat in it.

(chair ducks down and pops up next to Mama)

Mama: *(sniffs chair)* Ewww! My chair smells odd too! Like a little girl sat in it.

(chair ducks down and a pile of stick pops up next to Baby)

Baby: *(sniffles, crying)* At least you can still sit in your chairs. Someone sat in mine and broke it. Now all I have is a pile of sticks! Boo-hoo! *(pile of sticks ducks down)*

Papa: This is terrible! We have an intruder!

Mama: Search the house! *(all three bears rush offstage, then peek over the edge of the stage as snoring sounds come from offstage)*

Narrator: The three bears searched the main floor and then went upstairs to see if anyone was hiding in the bedroom.

Papa: Do you hear that! I think someone is sleeping up here.

Mama: Let's check it out! *(all three bears pop up, along with an empty bed next to Papa)*

Papa: Hmm . . . my bed is empty — but the blankets are ruffled. Someone's definitely tried sleeping in it.

(bed ducks down and pops up again next to Mama)

Mama: *(sniffing bed)* My bed is empty too — but it smells like my chair downstairs. Someone definitely tried sleeping in it.

(bed ducks down and then pops back up with Goldilocks in it)

Baby: *(looks down at bed)* Well, I know for a fact that someone has been sleeping in my bed . . . because she is still in it! AAAHHH!

(all three bears loom over Goldilocks)

Goldilocks: *(waking up)* YAWN! Oh, my! Did I fall asleep?

Goldilocks: *(realizes bears are looking at her)*
EEEKK! Don't eat me! AHHHH!
(hops out of bed)

Papa: *(blocks Goldilocks on one side)* Oh, don't worry. We're not going to eat you.

Goldilocks: *(shaking, scared)* You're not?

Mama: *(blocks Goldilocks on the other side, pinning her in)* We're going to do much worse, young lady. We're taking you home to your mother so you can explain just what you've been up to today!

Golidlocks: Oh, no! Not my mother! *(hangs her head)*

(all three bears guide Goldilocks offstage)

Baby: You're in trouble!

The End

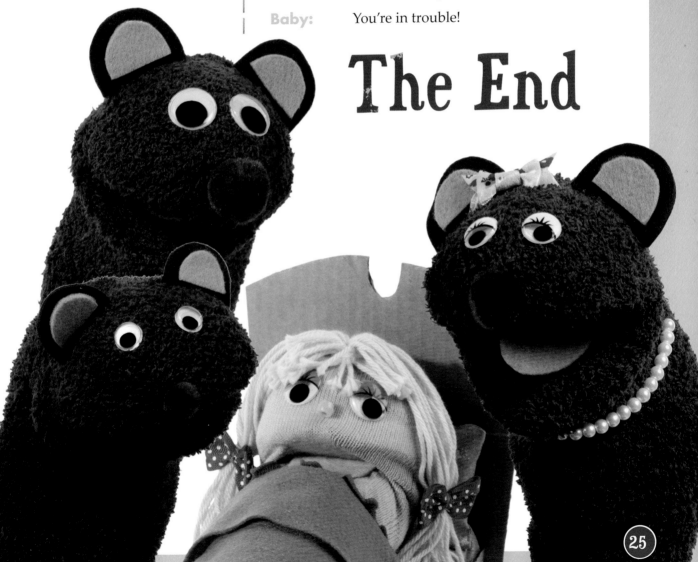

Take the Stage!

Your puppets, props, and stage are ready to go. You've even read the script a dozen times. Are you and your friends all set to put on a show? Almost! But before the big performance, keep these tips in mind to make your show shine!

Create Voices

Listen to the voices of everyone you know. Do they sound the same? Probably not. Just like everyone in the real world, your puppets should have their own voices too. Think about the characters, and play with voices that fit them best. For example, maybe Goldilocks has a sassy voice to match her naughty behavior. Meanwhile, maybe the bears have different voices to match their ages and genders.

Develop Personalities

Puppets need personalities. Each character in your play should act, move, and speak in its own unique way. Try these ideas for giving your puppets personality:

• Is Goldilocks afraid someone is going to discover her misbehaving in the bears' home? If so, have her look over her shoulders before she eats the porridge or sits on the chairs.

• Does Baby Bear get super-sad when his porridge is gone and his chair is broken? Consider having him hang his head and cry when he makes these discoveries.

• Move the puppets in ways that show their surprise. Tilt the bears' heads and open their mouths wide when they discover Goldilocks asleep in bed. Doing so will make them look confused and shocked at the same time.

Plan Your Movements

Your puppets need to move around and act out the action during the play. Decide ahead of time what they should do. For instance, how does Goldilocks sits on the chairs? Does she do so gently, or does she treat them roughly? And how should Mama and Papa Bear act when they sniff their furniture and catch a whiff of Goldilocks?

Practice the Play

To perform a great show, you need to practice it first. Run through your play several times before showing it to a real audience. The more you practice, the better your performance will be.

Before you know it, you'll be a puppet show pro!

The Show Must Go On!

You've performed *Goldilocks and the Three Bears* and everyone loved the show! Time to pack away the puppets, right? Not yet! Use your experience to get really creative. Try these fun ideas for changing your play or planning a new one:

Plan a sequel. Write a new play script that shows Baby Bear sneaking into Goldilocks' house. Is he on a payback or peacekeeping mission?

Make Goldilocks into a ninja or a spy. Rewrite her dialogue in a way that explains why she is in the bears' home. What does she hope to accomplish on her secret mission?

Change the props. What would happen if Goldilocks ate Brussels sprouts instead of porridge? What if she tried out Baby Bear's bicycle instead of his chair? Just imagine the kinds of trouble she could get into!

Rewrite the ending. What would happen if Goldilocks hid under the bed when the bears came home? Would they still find her? What would they do if she got away? Give your tale's ending an unexpected twist.

Conclusion

Now that you've mastered *Goldilocks and the Three Bears*, what comes next? Luckily the world is full of fables, fairy tales, and myths. Pick a story you like, and use your new skills to make your own puppets. Your next great sock puppet performance is in your hands!

Glossary

audience (AW-dee-uhns)—people who watch or listen to a play, movie, or show

character (KAYR-ik-tuhr)—a person or creature in a story

dialogue (DYE-uh-lawg)—the words spoken between two or more characters

imagination (i-maj-uh-NAY-shuhn)—the ability to form pictures in your mind of things that are not present or real

invade (in-VADE)—to enter a building, area, or country in order to take control of it

performance (pur-FOR-muhnss)—the public presentation of a play, movie, or piece of music

personality (pur-suh-NAL-uh-tee)—all of the qualities or traits that make one person different from others

porridge (POOR-ij)—a creamy, hot cereal

production (pruh-DUHK-shuhn)—a play or any form of entertainment that is presented to others

prop (PROP)—an item used by an actor or performer during a show

rehearsal (ri-HURSS-uhl)—a practice performance of a script

script (SKRIPT)—the story for a play, movie, or television show

tension rod (TEN-shuhn ROD)—a curtain rod that can be adjusted to fit snuggly in a window frame or doorframe

Read More

Kandel, Tiger, and Heather Schloss. *The Ultimate Sock Puppet Book: Clever Tips, Tricks, and Techniques for Creating Imaginative Sock Puppets.* Minneapolis: Creative Publishing International, 2014.

Petelinsek, Kathleen. *Making Sock Puppets.* How-to Library. Ann Arbor, Mich.: Cherry Lake Publishing, 2015.

Reynolds, Toby. *Making Puppets.* Mini Artist. New York: Windmill Books, 2016.

Internet Sites

Use FactHound to find Internet sites related to this book.

Visit *www.facthound.com*

Just type in 9781515766810 and go.

 Check out projects, games and lots more at **www.capstonekids.com**

Maker Space Tips

Download tips and tricks for using this book and others in a library maker space.

Visit *www.capstonepub.com/dabblelabresources*

TITLES IN THIS SET:

Goldilocks and the Three Bears
A Make and Play Production
by Christopher Harbo

Little Red Riding Hood
A Make and Play Production
by Christopher Harbo

The Three Billy Goats Gruff
A Make and Play Production
by Christopher Harbo

The Three Little Pigs
A Make and Play Production
by Christopher Harbo